S0-AQH-203

DUE

Christmas Traditions in Latin America
Tradiciones navideñas de Latinoamérica

Kerrie Logan Hollihan

**Traducción al español:
Ma. Pilar Sanz**

PowerKiDS press & **Editorial Buenas Letras**™
New York

For Meredith, who loves Christmas

Published in 2010 by The Rosen Publishing Group, Inc.
29 East 21st Street, New York, NY 10010

First Edition

Editor: Nicole Pristash
Book Design: Greg Tucker
Photo Researcher: Jessica Gerweck

Photo Credits: Cover, p. 17 Stan Honda/AFP/Getty Images; p. 5 © www.iStockphoto.com/Carmen Martínez Banús; p. 7 © SuperStock; p. 9 © John Dominis/age fotostock; p. 11 Yellow Dog Productions/Getty Images; p. 13 © Leonardo Diaz Romero/age fotostock; p. 15 Bruce Ayres/Getty Images; p. 19 Ariel Skelley/Getty Images; p. 21 Yamini Chao/Getty Images.

Library of Congress Cataloging-in-Publication Data

Hollihan, Kerrie Logan.
  Christmas traditions in Latin America = Tradiciones navideñas de Latinoamérica / Kerrie Logan Hollihan ; traducción al español, Ma. Pilar Sanz. — 1st ed.
    p. cm. — (Latin American celebrations and festivals = Celebraciones y festivales de Latinoamérica)
  Includes bibliographical references and index.
  ISBN 978-1-4358-9365-8 (library binding)
  1. Christmas—Latin America—Juvenile literature. 2. Latin America—Social life and customs—Juvenile literature. I. Title. II. Title: Tradiciones navideñas de Latinoamérica.
  GT4987.155.H65 2010
  394.2663098—dc22
                                        2009031044

Manufactured in the United States of America

CPSIA Compliance Information: Batch #WW10PK: For Further Information contact Rosen Publishing, New York, New York at 1-800-237-9932

CONTENTS

CONTENIDO

Many families in Latin America are very busy in December. They are preparing to **celebrate** Christmas, or the day Jesus was born. In Latin America, the Christmas season is called *la Navidad* (nah-vee-THAHD). Many people take time to make these special days full of joy.

En toda Latinoamérica, las familias tienen mucho que hacer en diciembre. Todos se preparan para **celebrar** las fiestas de Navidad, o el día del nacimiento de Jesucristo. Durante la Navidad muchas personas toman el tiempo para celebrar estos días llenos de paz y alegría.

Many Latinos prepare for la Navidad by decorating their homes.

Muchos latinos decoran sus casas para celebrar la Navidad.

Las Posadas (poh-SAH-thahs) is a nine-day celebration that many Mexicans and other Latinos take part in during la Navidad. It begins on December 16 and ends on December 24. Las Posadas honors Joseph and Mary's search for a place for Jesus to be born.

Las posadas son una celebración de nueve días de duración que se lleva a cabo en México y otros países de Latinoamérica durante las fiestas navideñas. Las posadas comienzan el 16 de diciembre y terminan el 24 de diciembre. Las posadas recuerdan la jornada de María y José en busca del lugar en el que nacería Jesucristo.

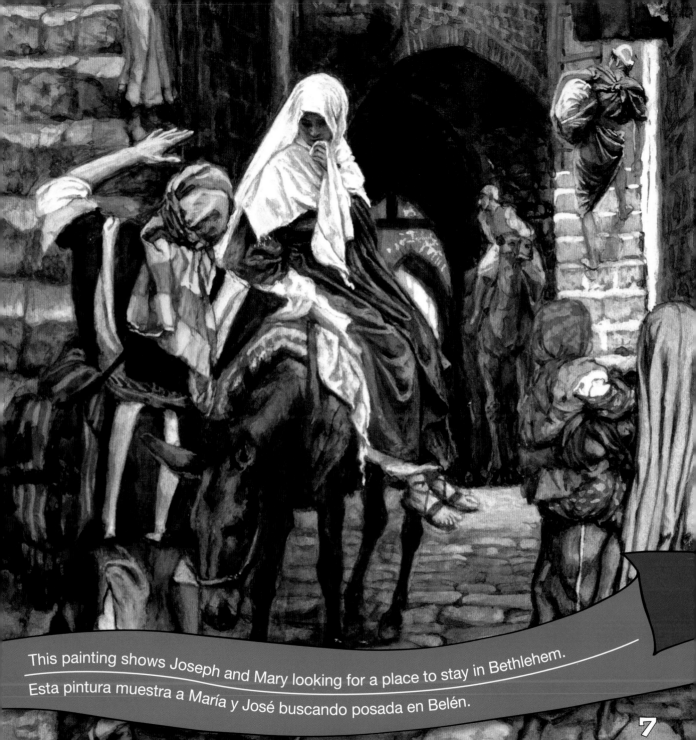

This painting shows Joseph and Mary looking for a place to stay in Bethlehem.

Esta pintura muestra a María y José buscando posada en Belén.

During the celebration, children and adults play the parts of Joseph and Mary as they seek a room in a posada, or **inn**. Joseph and Mary knock on the door while singing. Innkeepers welcome them. Inside, a party waits. Everyone sings, eats, and children hit a **piñata**.

Durante las posadas, niños y adultos recrean la búsqueda de una posada, o **mesón**, de María y José. María y José tocan a la puerta cantando. Otros invitados, haciendo de posaderos, les dan la bienvenida y los invitan a pasar. Más tarde se hace una fiesta. Todos bailan, cantan y le pegan a la **piñata**.

Las Posadas is a fun celebration. People sing, eat, and hit piñatas, as this boy is doing.

Las posadas son una celebración muy divertida. La gente canta, come y rompe piñatas.

9

During la Navidad, many families build *nacimientos* (nah-sih-mee-EN-tohs), or models of the **stable** in which Jesus was born. They add figures of Mary and Joseph inside of it. Then, children place the baby Jesus in his bed on *la nochebuena* (NOH-chay BWAY-nah), or Christmas Eve.

Durante la Navidad las familias ponen nacimientos, o modelos del **establo**, en el que nació Jesucristo. En los nacimientos se colocan figuras de María y José. Durante la nochebuena, el 24 de diciembre, los chicos ponen una figura del niño Jesús en su cuna.

This girl is placing the baby Jesus in his bed inside the nacimiento on Christmas Eve.

Esta niña está poniendo al bebé Jesús en el nacimiento durante la nochebuena.

Christmas Eve is celebrated differently across Latin America. Many families go to church. Ecuador's people count down the minutes until midnight, the time that Jesus was thought to have been born. Puerto Ricans and Dominicans sing songs. Many Latin American children open gifts.

La nochebuena es celebrada en toda Latinoamérica. Muchas familias van a la iglesia. En Ecuador la gente cuenta los minutos hasta la medianoche, que es cuando se cree que nació Jesús. En Puerto Rico y la República Dominicana la gente canta. Muchos chicos en Latinoamérica abren regalos en la nochebuena.

During la Navidad, many buildings in Latin America are decorated with lights.

Muchos edificios en Latinoamérica se decoran con muchas luces durante la Navidad.

13

On Christmas Day, many families feast on turkey, ham, and special **tamales**. Puerto Ricans eat *pasteles* (pahs-TEL-es), tamales cooked in banana leaves. Mexican children munch on cookies called *biscochitos* (bee-skoh-CHEE-tohs). Panamanians enjoy rice with pineapple.

El día de Navidad, muchas familias festejan comiendo pavo y **tamales** especiales para la celebración. Los puertorriqueños comen pasteles, o tamales cocidos en hojas de plátano. En México, muchos chicos comen galletas llamadas bizcochitos. En Panamá, se come arroz con piña.

Coming together to eat with family and friends is an important part of la Navidad.

Reunirse para comer con los amigos y la familia es una parte importante de la Navidad.

Los tres Reyes magos (TREHS RAY-es MAH-gohs), or the Three Wise Men, play an important part in la Navidad. The Three Wise Men are said to have been kings who brought gifts to the baby Jesus. This visit is celebrated on January 6. Many Latin American children receive gifts on this day.

Los tres Reyes magos juegan un papel muy importante durante la celebración de la Navidad. La historia nos dice que los tres Reyes magos le llevaron regalos al niño Jesús. Esta visita se celebra el 6 de enero. Muchos niños en Latinoamérica reciben regalos ese día.

These people dressed up for a parade celebrating the Three Wise Men.

Estas personas se visten como los tres Reyes magos durante un desfile.

In Puerto Rico, many children place boxes of grass under their beds on the night of January 5. They believe that this grass is for the Three Wise Mens' camels to eat. When the children wake up in the morning, they may find presents where the grass once was!

Muchos niños en Puerto Rico ponen cajas con hierba debajo de sus camas en la noche del 5 de enero. Se cree que esta hierba es para que el camello de los tres Reyes magos pueda comer. ¡A la mañana siguiente, los chicos encuentran regalos dentro de las cajas!

Opening gifts is a tradition in Latin America during la Navidad.

Abrir regalos es otra tradición durante la Navidad en Latinoamerica.

19

Latin Americans bake special bread called rosca de reyes (ROH-skah DAY RAY-es), or bread of kings, for *el Día* (DEE-uh) *de los tres Reyes magos*. This bread is ring-shaped and filled with dried fruits and nuts. Everyone enjoys a piece with cups of hot chocolate.

En Latinoamérica se prepara un pan muy especial para celebrar el día de los Reyes magos. A este pan se le llama rosca de reyes. La rosca de reyes tiene forma de anillo y está decorada con fruta seca y nueces. La rosca de reyes se disfruta mucho con una taza de chocolate caliente.

Adding fruit to rosca de reyes, shown here, makes this bread very sweet!

La fruta en la rosca de reyes le da un sabor dulce. ¡Deliciosa!

Christmas is a special time in Latin America. Many people take time to celebrate the birth of Jesus and to honor Joseph, Mary, and the Three Wise Men. Families and friends come together and wish each other a *¡Feliz Navidad!* (fel-EES nah-vee-THAHD), or Merry Christmas!

La Navidad es una época muy especial en Latinoamérica. Muchas personas celebran el nacimiento de Jesucristo y honran a María, José y los tres Reyes magos. La familias y amigos se reúnen para desear a todos una ¡Feliz Navidad!

Glossary

celebrate (SEH-leh-brayt) To honor an important moment by doing special things.

inn (IN) A place where travelers can get food and a place to sleep.

piñata (peen-YAH-tuhs) A special container filled with candies that children break with sticks.

stable (STAY-bul) A building in which farm animals are kept and fed.

tamales (tuh-MAH-leez) Dishes made of corn dough that are stuffed with certain things.

Glosario

celebrar Festejar un momento importante haciendo cosas especiales.

establo (el) Un edificio en una granja en el que se albergan los animales.

mesón (el) Un lugar en el que los viajeros pueden comer y dormir.

piñata (la) Un recipiente especial que se llena de dulces y que los niños y niñas rompen con un palo.

tamales (los) Un platillo realizado con masa de maíz rellenos de carne o verduras.

Index

Índice

Web Sites / Páginas de Internet

Due to the changing nature of Internet links, PowerKids Press has developed an online list of Web sites related to the subject of this book. This site is updated regularly. Please use this link to access the list:
www.powerkidslinks.com/LACF/christmas/